AF390953

POEMS

R.P.I. – LO–O7-2020-210

Pencil, paper and words.

Pencil, paper and words.
ISBN: 9798595428385
Legal deposit: LO–O7-2020-210
First edition: January 2021
Independently published

ÍNDICE

Analogies

If by analogy is understood,
similarity relationship
between very different things.

If between good and bad
there are analogies.

If between the just and unjust
there are analogies.

If among all the materials,
even in their different types,
stone, metal, plastic,
textile... analogies can be found.

If between opposite ideas
sometimes antagonistic,
there are always analogies.

Why do us almost always
insist on enlarging the differences
and dwarfing the similarities?

<u>Hurricane</u>

Hurricane with own name,
that all place where you pass,
you raze with extreme speed,
that the trees pull off
and by the air you raise them,
like sea gull feathers,
transported by wind.

Everything that in your path
it is interposed, you destroy.
Into a thousand shattered pieces,
that on mounds unusable like funeral pyres,
they is piled up,
when from the sky they fall.

The sea water you rise
with heights of giant magnitudes,
that flood everything they find on mainland,
with immeasurable strength,
razing everything,
what they find in its path.

Winds that change everything,
nothing left in place;
the straight makes it curved,
or they split it if it doesn't bend.
If the wind keeps blowing
at lightning speed, it will be
because his name has changed,
with a simple adjective, hurricane.

The water that falls to the floor,
like stones of great weight,
does not fall but it is collapsed at vertigo speed
and it is become rivers,
that everything that settles in its path,
drags it.

Short is the time
what its violence lasts,
if we compare it
with the time needed
to fix and rebuild everything
what to its step has destroyed.

<u>Depression</u>

Words that distill sadness, dejection
and lack of illusion,
in a folio, they have been written.

Depressive moods reflect that,
in the fog they take refuge,
preventing seeing the sun.

Words, which to the heart shrink
and when you hear them, they denote,
that shouting, help are asking,
in the form of love, affection, friendship
or just attention.

The incomprehension
of a concretionary reality,
with the certainty of the suffering caused,
provokes the rebellion.

How to channel that sadness
and disquiet?
It is a question of difficult solution.

Perhaps, the passage of time;

driving away loneliness,

to feel part of something,

discover new perspectives,

that negative feelings take away,

and the warmth of sun,

comes near us.

Today and yesterday

Does time advance

to the rhythm of harmony

that the sounds of nature dictate to it?

Fulminating time of hurricane winds,

and gusts of lightning.

Where yesterday disappears

and becomes today

in an infinite circle.

No brake stops it

until its cycle ends.

Memory of yesterday's time,

the water has oxidized it

and the wind has razed it away.

Yesterday's world has been transformed

in an unreal memory,

multifaceted and changeable.

Only the instant,

the moment of the today,

remains more real, objective,

and less contaminated by imagination,

that feelings rise and drop,

like giant waves

from an enraged sea,

by gusty winds.

If a calm sea,

it's living today's time,

enjoying the second,

aware that time

is changing, cyclic,

which drags everything

in its path he reaches,

and in the yesterday deposits it.

Why is the today so short,

and why always

in the yesterday, it accumulates?

<u>Diversity</u>

Flowers that from the ground sprout.
Seeds from which you are born.
Diversity that your blends amplify
and the variety in the world increase.

A time when everything multiplies,
and where there were a hundred
there are now a thousand.
Changes that expand it everything
and its size enlarge.

Advances that, after failed tests,
achieve their objectives.

Roses, granddaughters of other roses,
but with the smell to daisies
and size of giant hydrangeas.

Oranges with the skin of lemons,
and the size of melons,
the taste of cherries
and the life of the quinces.

Men with metallic heart,
the legs of a gazelle
and arms that on two giant wings unfold.

Robots, with human feelings,
and extreme sensitivity,
in a bodies without soul.

<u>Childhood and love</u>

Retain the hand
that my cheek caresses,
that on my head with love she places
and my hair she kisses.
My whole being feels
the love that it transmits to me.

Children who have never felt,
the warmth of a caress.
Neither hand her love
transmitted to them.

Children who don't feel loved
because they've never felt
the caresses and kisses
that accompany love.

How does grows
and behaves a child,
who has not received love?

What influence does
 the absence of love
has on the development
of the brain?

The path

One cold January day
the road began,
without knowing how it would elapse,
the duration it was going to have
nor where and how it would end.

Long and painful days,
along with other short and happy,
the path he was traveling.

As the road progressed,
very diverse people he met,
and everyone contributed him something.
He enjoyed the good
and from the bad, he learned
to try to avoid it.

Several rivers on his way he crossed,
in each one of them
his reflected image saw.
At first, he is scared,
because his image changed a lot
in each river that crossed.

River by river he understood
that as he advanced
his life is shortened.

Guide dogs

Light that leads to time,

like a dog to a blind man

who guides him with his eyes,

and from dangers saves him,

giving security to his life.

Love, what in exchange for very little,

with exaggeration extreme

he gives in excess.

Warmth, that as a powerful light source

his company brings.

Mutual attraction which,

like the honey to flies,

his company incites

and stimulates the awakening.

His leisurely and safe walking,

every second marks him,

to the beat of the baton

that the compasses of the security,

they mark to him.

His soft, slow and calm steps,

like a relaxed tempo

that transports us to the dream;

to the eyelids he closes it

and to us he wraps

in a blanket of feathers;

light but warm,

which from the bustle isolates us.

Why a small animal can give much more

than many human beings?

<u>Shapes</u>

Forms or appearances that,
in the eyes of who looks them,
have all the things
that our vision reaches.

Stable forms,
whose silhouettes remain
throughout the ages.
Distinguishing them is very easy,
since few variations suffer.

Human shape silhouettes,
animal silhouettes,
that with very little effort
the brain recognizes,
and even gives it a name
and its full figure,
with just glimpse them shape.

Form or identity of each thing,
the same an object as a living being,
with a pencil we copy it
and its shape we draw,
joining a few lines
with their corresponding shadows.

Shadows that sunlight creates,
without the need for a pencil,
and a thousand shapes it gives away us.

Defend itself

Defend itself from the cold
with thick clothes
or in a warm shelter.

Take shelter from the rain,
under a roof that protects us.

Protect oneself from the wind
that with unusual strength,
us body drags it,
as if a cardboard image were.

Defend oneself from the heat with water,
which on the outside and inside refreshes us.

Taking refuge us on rest,
when the tiredness,
to shouts, is warning you.

Defending oneself from routines,
with unexpected things,
that our habits change,
when discovering other new horizons.

Defend against our own violence
or uncontrolled anger,
with calm, control and respect.

Safeguard us from the manipulation
that they throw us every day,
taking us aware of it.

Protecting us from false truths
or half-truths,
same as of the lies.

Agitation

Agitation that the spirit alter;
bombardment of negative news,
insistent, almost all pessimistic,
that the thought they direct it,
infecting it as a virus
that is incubated in an organism,
and its functioning changes
with sickly symptoms.

Contrasting its symptoms
with impartially and sense.
Doesn't letting itself be dragged
by the stormy wind of the unreason,
that with the disease
the virus has incubated.

Counteract its symptoms,
with right medication and cares.
Fight them with common sense
and knowledge of the past,
which almost always eliminate them.

Get away from the contagious source,
where the virus is installed.
Looking for healthy environments
where the germ doesn't rule too much,
and the organism, little by little,
in a stress-free environment,
agitations and clashes, likewise, it is relax.

The river returns to its course,
with calm movements,
which by the names
of dialogue and wisdom we know,
advancing towards its sea.

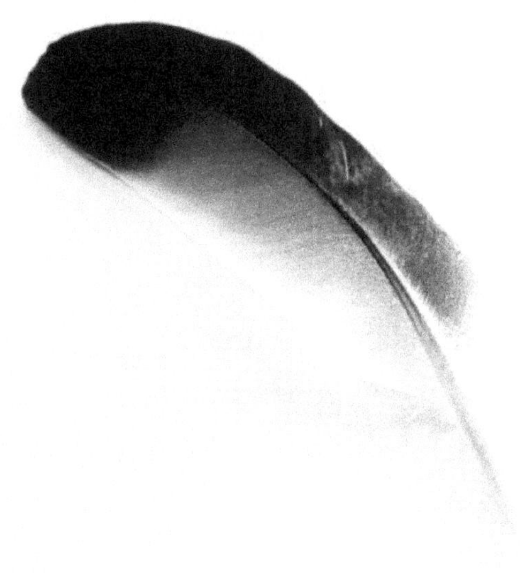

Scarecrow

A big scarecrow
made of rag,
with several clothes it is covered,
in the middle of the farm,
it is planted.

Years go happening,
and just like a clock marks the hours,
its four seasons are succeeding each other,
one after another, always the same,
on their tanned skin, they are engraved.

The traces that the lapse of the time is leaving,
in the scarecrow accumulate,
and one by one,
shreds of his body they are tearing,
thus altering its essence.

The birds no longer fear him,
since his figure is already
part of the environment,
and each time with more rage,
its life they tear out .

Its figure the time has transformed,

now it is small, thin,

weak and very hunched over.

An autumn, the rain, the wind

and the cold to the ground have thrown it.

The trees, their faithful neighbors,

with their leaves,

his body have covered it.

Conflict

How can one know what doesn't exist?
How can forget something
that is ignored?

But if it is could know
something that didn't exist before,
and if it existed, it was ignored,
for not understanding it
and letting it be.

But if we would remember us of some of the
things who we ignore
and we will try to decipher them.

For the one who ignore,
the ignored it does not exist.
But if the non-existent
suddenly becomes visible,
ignoring it is very difficult,
because in everyone's eyes,
it has been shown.

Once the nonexistent or ignored,

with the force of light, becomes visible,

from far away it can see it.

How will is your vision?

It will look the same

from the four cardinal points.

It's likely, at a minimum,

we´ll let's have four points of view

depending on the place, from which we see it.

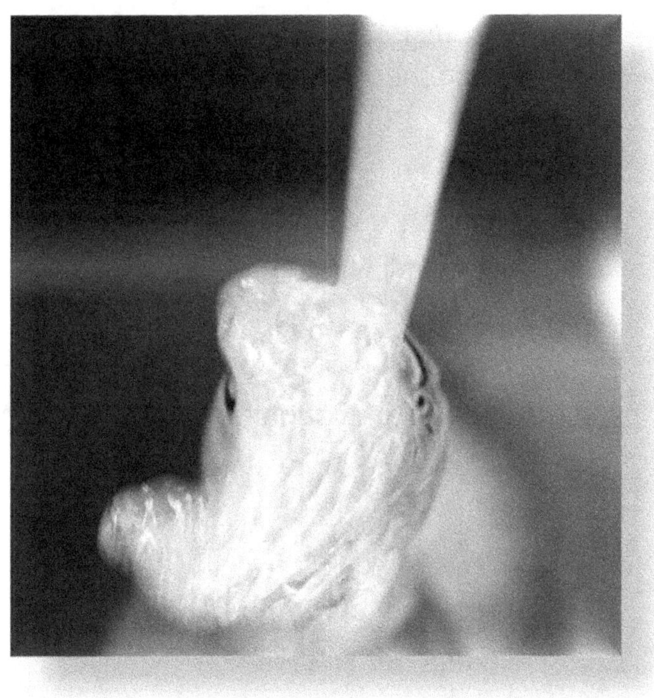

<u>Empathy</u>

Your sadness in my brain
is embedded,
without me having any reason for it.

I feel it as if it were mine.
If to you it makes cry
without knowing why, I cry.

Your dejection and apathy
I perceive with such intensity,
feeling them like mine.

Your pain I do not feel it,
but all my schemes is broken
if I can't alleviate it.

Your joy, me of joy floods.
If you laugh I laugh too.
If you dance I move to your beat.

Why, many times,
a reality of others,
we feel her so close?

<u>Falling off</u>

To a big and old stone,
a giant foot, embedded
in a boot of fire,
a kick has given to her.

The stone, which time has worn away
and round and smooth is has stayed;
ready and willing it is.
If from a slope, she falls,
in her descent it will drag infinity of
stones of much smaller size.

Many of them, being small,
 in the fall, they will break.
Others will disappear embedded in the earth,
turned into sand.
The big stone, which its fall caused,
with high probability, little damaged it will result.

Little by little, step by step,
higher velocity it is taking.
For the slope she goes down,
razing everything that in her way
is interposed.

If the size of the stone increases
for thousand beings, adhered,
her damage will be proportional
to their size increasing.

The living beings that their fall they intuit,
with great speed, they flee.
Escaping from the avalanche
that the great stone provokes,
it is something instinctive,
in everything that has life.

The great stone, in its descent,
is going dragging smaller ones,
which accompany its fall.
Upon reaching the plain, their journey is over.

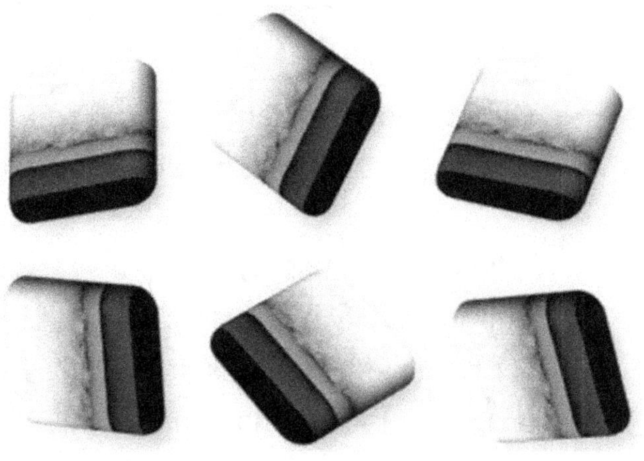

Ambiguities

It's not cold today, but it's not hot either.

The number eight is real
or they are two zeros that the wind
has united them and can separate them.

This pants that is broken,
is because it is very abraded,
or because fashion has imposed it
and it's still not has worn?

Everything is full, but full of emptiness.
He cries because he's sad or he cries for joy.

He ran and ran and never arrived
because him always ran.

The car circulated so slowly
that it was always filled of snails.

A child grew so much every year,
who always wore a cloud by hat.

A sportsman threw the ball so hard
that was incrusted in an apple tree.
After several years the apples
acquired the shape of a ball,
and on the ground they played.

<u>Old age</u>

A man, step by step, he walks.
The time, second to second,
in his life is passing.
Sometimes the joy in your life
with various forms is installed.
Others times the sadness,
in very different degrees,
in his heart he feels it.
The activity with periods of inactivity,
a constant as day and night,
in his life they gone alternated.

A man, who mentally walks,
him thinks and imagines
without the need to walk.
Images of a past time,
in his memory he keeps them.
These are always different,
according to the time what,
to them, represent,
childhood, youth, maturity...

Time stops in an image,
but if with the remembrance,
to more images we join it,
the time, we will lengthen it.

The man when he reaches old age,
step by step, he continues to walk.
His time, second to second passes,
but his steps are slower,
and his time lengthens it,
with images of his past.
Images that sometimes,
he feels them more near,
by reliving them in his memory,
than the time of today present.

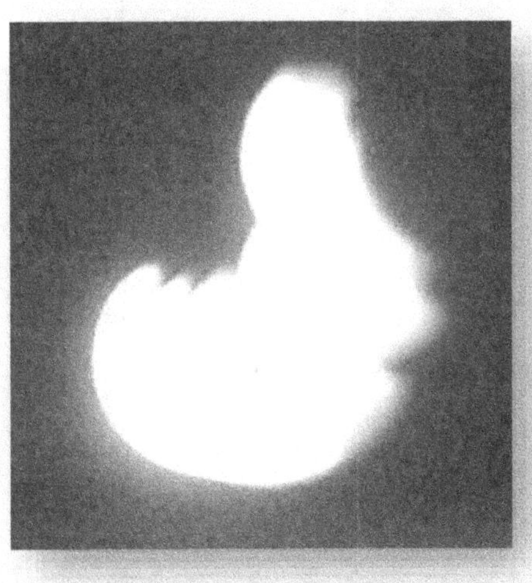

Flying

Flies a bird over the sky
towards far confines,
traveling new skies
ignored for others.

Flies a child's imagination,
discovering new worlds
that rational reality does not reach,
unless you are a child.

Flies the sand of the sea
by the wind transported,
when its trip is over,
a new life begins.

Fly the leaves of a tree,
when autumn appears.
On the land they settle
and their matter transform.

Flies a balloon through space
until its air runs out,
and on the ground it falls
or in the sky it explodes.

Flies a sound through the air,
strong and loud; while he walks away
its echo is becoming weaker and weaker,
until with silence it integrates.

Present

Day by day, year after year,
with the gaze puts
on the top of a hill,
little by little, he always ascended,
and never his sight of the top diverted it.

After many years,
when more than half life,
he had already spent,
one night, from a dream, he woke up,
from his eyes a blindfold fell
and his mind understood.

Having always your eyes
on an imaginary peak,
that he wanted to achieve,
his whole life it conditioned.

Then he understood,
by remembering the images,
that from all his past life,
he kept in his brain.

That he never enjoyed
and never bothered about stopping
on the path, and enjoy the present,
by conditioning your being,
with the vision always active
of a future and nonexistent peak.

Music

If music has meaning,
without needing words.

If love is given and received
even if there are no words.

Friendship goes beyond of words.

Joy is felt without needing words.

Sadness is joined with tears
better than it does with words.

It doesn't need words
to feel happiness.

Sentiments which all person,
receives and transmits.

To the sentiments of others it is receptive,
without needing words,
only perceives them
and they are part of her.

Music with words
or music without words.

Stepping on the ground
or floating on it.

<u>Perception</u>

A picture on a wall, hang.
Thousands of photographs of it
have been taken.

All the photos the same image
have captured, although the years
have been happening.

Two people observe the same picture.
One sees in the picture a river,
the other sees a path.

One sees three trees together and different,
the other sees a mountain far way.

One sees three human figures,
the other sees a human figure,
a big dog and a motorbike.

Both affirm and assure
that their vision is the real one.

If a photograph of the picture
would be regaled to them?

Their vision would remain the same,
without changing anything of anything?

The vision that our eyes capture
and our brain processes
in each human being it is different,
according to we want to see it,
and to us satisfy.

Joy and sadness

Sadness which, like the fog,
to a human being you surround
and in darkness you install it.

Sadness, which through soft and warm tears,
that from your eyes fall,
to your anguish they soften it.

Sadness to which a logical and positive
reasoning, like a tropical and gentle wind,
it moves away from your head.

Joy which to sadness you surround,
with very varied shapes;
with a thousand merry disguises,
with which to sadness you dress,
because the effect of contagion
almost always arises effect.

Joy which to sadness you wrap
and make spin like a spinning top
which in the end always
by its own weight falls.

Joy dressed of rainbow
putting ending the dark gray of sadness,
like when a storm passes.

<u>Impotence</u>

"Mommy, I want water",
a boy shouts.

His mother spins around nervous,
doesn't know what to answer.

From his eyes tears of water sprout
but she can't give them to him.

Due to her helplessness,
more tears from his eyes sprout.

His mother, very nervous
about this situation,
takes an apple among your hands,
and with immense love
and a warm smile,
she gives it the child.

Eat you this apple
that contains fresh and good water.

<u>Trees</u>

Trees, of birds your home,
shelter and warmth in their lives.
Leaf tiles that to their bodies protect.
Families that in their branches
their ties intertwine.

Colors that dress the tree
throughout their lives,
although its essence doesn't change.

Birds that on the branches of a tree,
their small bodies swing
to the rhythm of the movement
of its oscillating leaves.

Trees filled with birds
like inhabited houses,
with lighted chimneys
and musical sounds.

Trees without leaves or birds
that to their warmth they take refuge.
Like abandoned houses
whose lives disappear,
in a sea without movement.

Action or inaction

Cold that shrinks the body
and turns it into a ball,
folded on himself,
unable of movement.

The teeth like castanets,
rhythmically are moved.
The body trembles like a leaf
at the mercy of a strong wind.

In a corner he huddles up, stuck to a wall
that some protection give him.
There is no wind,
but his whole being trembles.

Little by little, his feet no longer he feels them,
like two blocks of ice
that they belonged to another nature,
incapable of movement.

Moving his hands hard work turns out,
motionless, as if they were made of marble,
him doesn't feel,
that they are part of their body yet.

Making a great effort,
not getting himself carried away
by the quietness of the minimum effort,
which would provoke his body to freeze.

He finally gets to move,
walk to slow motion,
obligating that his body to perform
all kinds of actions,
and his mind wake up.

Stay still in a corner
without action or movements,
leaving the mind in blank.
Or perform actions and movements
that our mind activates.

Discover

Armored doors,

to a large majority closed,

hard to cross,

but never impossible.

Because every door has as purpose,

passing from one world to another,

sometimes very similar,

other times different,

with languages of very distinct roots.

Simple doors of natural wood,

of very different types,

as many as kinds of wood

what exist in nature.

Go through them all we know,

because the effort is minimal.

We almost always open them with some will,

the number of doors we go through

will vary greatly from one person to another,

depending on the type of life,

which we have led.

Sometimes, we will pass on to a better world,
other times to different worlds,
unknown to us,
to which we will have to adapt.
With other doors we will go backwards
instead of advancing

Many times we will regret
having crossed that door,
and on our footsteps we will go back.
But if there's one thing we've learned,
it's that walking is advancing.

<u>Imaginary world</u>

Waking up from a distant dream,
in an imaginary world,
many times longed for,
but always unattainable.

Comfort is the queen.
No one feels strange.
Everything is adapted to the measure
of each being that inhabits it.

The differences do not exist
because they cannot be seen,
not even feel.

As if a puzzle were,
everything fits effortlessly.
For subsistence nothing is needed,
because everything we have it
in this ideal world,
where nothing is longed for
because nothing is desired.

All those who inhabit it in
of thousand unequal ways,
with a thousand different minds,
they live together in harmony.
Their relationship is perfect
because they don't feel nor see
that exist the differences.

In this imaginary world
many are the beings that live,
but his understanding is perfect
without the need to talk,
because exist no words
in different languages.

The language that is used
is the language mental,
the empathy and the love,
that to all unites them and equals them
in a world that belongs to everyone,
although it's really nobody's,
we only use it for a determinate time.

<u>Routines</u>

Vespers of parties: agitation,
preparation, movement, acceleration...
Vespers of events: stress,
nervousness, accumulated tension,
lack of sleep…

Why when the order of the routine is broken,
in the face of a different situation
or in spaced time, our mind is altered
and our body respond
with different symptoms?

Are we beings of fixed and
established customs?
Or the time of life in which we live,
set and determined on a specific date,
as inheritance it has left us,
specific schedules,
established routines,
in almost all our acts,
what stability they bring us?

Like a straight and wide road
with few curves in it,
what security gives us.

Are good these routines,
which make our lives easier
or simply more helpless make us,
at the face adversity
or different situations,
what stress they'll provoke us.

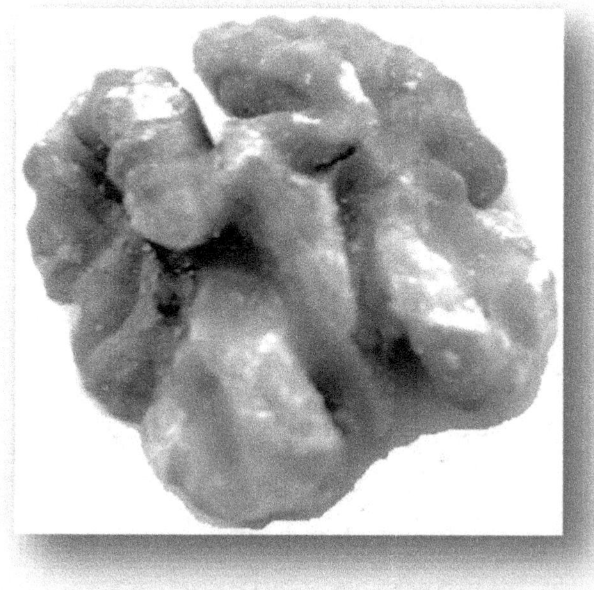

Musical language

In a place, in a very distant time,

inhabited a woman

with an unknown gift.

The words, which came out of her mouth,

are lengthened with different sizes,

at the same time that various musical sounds,

with the words were joined.

She didn't need orchestra that will join words

with different instruments.

The words with very different sounds

from his mouth emerged.

From all over the world

they came to listen,

the music with words

that his throat created.

And they were fascinated, because

all people from different countries

with their own languages,

their words understood.

The legend, from generation
to generation, it was transmitted,
until new legends
to the old ones were burying
in the well of oblivion.

<u>Simplify</u>

Why if everyone runs and walks,
I can't detach, my feet off the asphalt?
Why if he laughs and sings,
you in a dark corner cry?
Why if he eat and eat delicious delicacies,
you can't even a piece of bread chewing?

Why if he travel by land, sea and air
and his mind amplify
or sometimes simplifies,
you do not go out from a street?
Why if you talk and communicate
with a thousand different people,
he is dumb and deaf and in a bubble lives?

More if all this were false
and at the same time real.
If like a hand it were,
composed of two different parts,
if we look at the back of the hand,
we can't see the palm.

Harmony

A man walks down a street.
His way of walking his age shows us.
His back a long time ago
that it stopped being straight.
As a very curved arch,
it forces to tilt his head in excess,
incapable is of adopt a straight posture.
Not even his eyes can look straight ahead,
as he walks.

With one hand a solid cane holds,
that his safer walking allows him
and stability gives him.
With the other hand a dog leash subjects.
The dog to his walking,
along the way, adapts,
as an example of caring and adaptability,
worthy of imitation by any human being

The dog always does the same,
walks three steps and stops,
walks and stops,
while the old man, with steps slow
and very short, his walk quietly continues.

Adapt

Three children play with a rope.
It's a very old game,
than jumping to rope, they call it.
A child at each extreme
with his hands he hold it,
and to it they spin it around.
The third child jumps
and dodges the rope
as long as he can do it without falling.

The children that to the rope turn,
faster and faster do it,
so that the child falls
and one of them his position occupies.
This way they have fun
and places alternate.
Everyone jumps and spin the rope,
while the game continues.

A mother with a very small child
walks down a street.
The child very slowly walks,
because his legs are very small.

The mother her step adapts to the child's,
and very slowly she also walks.

A man with his little son,
take a bike ride.
The child for a short time has been riding,
and his balance is still precarious.
The father adapts to the child's rhythm
without him perceiving it,
and very slowly he pedals.

The child feels proud,
because at the same speed
that his father runs.

The child besides riding a bike
will learn to have confidence in himself,
and over time he will gain security.

Fitting to the new circumstances
is it something innate in people
or is it something that is learned
because it gives us stability?

<u>A leaf</u>

A leaf lies inert on the ground,
the time its color has stolen it,
its youth the air, has absorbed it,
and in a very different one,
it has been transformed.
Its form and its matter,
time slowly has been going changing it.

The wind with it plays
and where it wants it transports it,
up, down, right or left.
If it wants, and louder it blows,
it gyrates and spins around on itself.
When the wind of playing has got tired,
to the leaf on the ground, gently, deposits.

Time keeps moving forward,
and the leaf, little by little,
is transformed into dust,
which the wind blows back it
to different places where it deposit it,
in order that a different life begins.

Seasonal virus

Small and insignificant virus
than to giants attack.
His organism you invade
and his balance you collapse it,
like a house of cards.

Invisible and treacherous virus,
only your symptoms are visible
and detectable by anomalies.
Virus that change our routine,
against our wishes.

Contagious in excess
without us noticing it.
Any place is suitable,
as long as there are people,
who with him of the hand is promenaded,
although they have no conscience about it,
because sometimes he ignores it.

There are some that are very funny,
but it is better to remember
that they don't laugh like us,
their laugh is not ha ha ha ...
but cough, cough, cough...

<u>Everything changes</u>

A man for an unknown city, walks,
his steps travel it very slowly,
his eyes thousands of photos are taking
and he keeps them in his brain.

His ears, thousands of sounds distinguish,
of infinity of variants and classes.
Some for the first time he listens to them.
To all, with great care, he records them
and keeps them in his memory.

His nose, smells and aromas of many types
and intensity, perceive.
Some new ones for him, they turn out
and, unconsciously,
in a corner of his brain he deposits them.

The brain does not stop working
and everything agglutinates it and classifies
in several and very diverse groups.
Each group is different
because something is always different,
although existed similarities.

To all of them he groups
with the name of the city.

After many years,
the same man travels the same city,
and new thought groups he will form,
and to the old ones that his brain kept
in something will changed them.

Since, although the city is the same,
the images, sounds and smells
that he'll capture very different will be,
because something always changes in
everything, including our own brain
and our own memories.

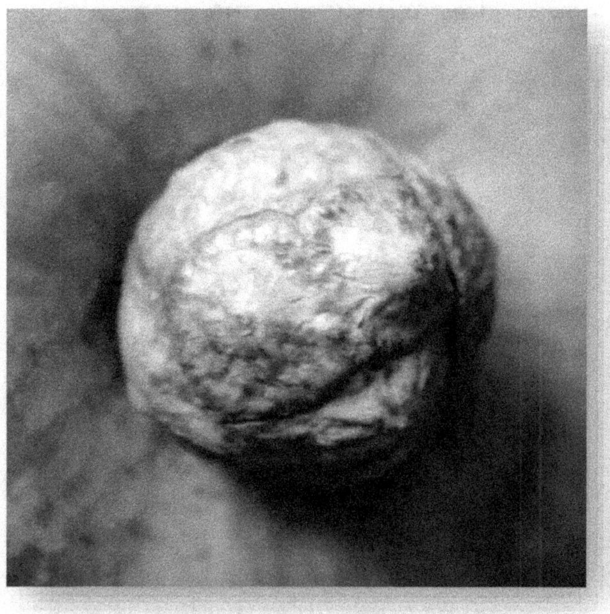

<u>Doors</u>

Doors that the entrance and exit
of places facilitate,
both physical and mental.

Doors that to places known
and sometimes unknown,
they facilitate us the passage.

Doors that bring us closer to knowledge,
discovering new worlds,
while the our they enlarge.

People who many doors have opened,
known or unknown,
throughout their lives,
and their world, they have changed
for better or worse.

People who almost no doors have crossed,
for comfort or simply ignore
who, in your mind,
many doors every day they could open.

Affinity

Tune an instrument
until its sound, to the ears
of people, better it sounds,
its sensitivity increases,
and the difference between various notes
is immediately perceived.

Its diversity of tones
to the refine them, we amplified it.
The affinity of various instruments,
coupled between them,
as a single sound we perceive it.

If harmonizing and having affinity
in various sounds we achieve
with various instruments.

If at cost of retouching,
correcting the necessary times,
we achieve the perfection.

Why among people,
is it sometimes so difficult,
to harmonize and have affinity?

Learning enjoying

A child when he's small,
with a paper and a pencil
his first drawings he traces.

With colored pencils
his drawings he colors.
In this simple way,
he discover the different colors
that life offers him.

As time goes by,
with a pencil and a paper
his first letters he learns,
and on the paper he writes them
very slowly at first.

A man all his life remembers,
what thanks to a pencil and a paper;
being a child and enjoying, he learned.

Pencil and paper

Pencil that a piece of paper you look for
as food pursues the hungry.
Words that is written on paper
to lighten the mind and put them on it.

Simple paper that for a thousand functions
you serve, with simplicity and purity.
Light as a feather, you resist well the years
if with love you are taken care of.

Paper doesn't know talk,
because listening is its destiny.
Where could one speak,
without complexes, without stress,
if it is not upon your white texture?

Paper that sadness and sorrows
of so many people you keep away,
when they're discharged them upon you,
lightening his conscience and soul.

Many times the joys and sayings
with ink are engraved, on the lonely paper
that very far can fly
and with others be shared,
although wings do not have.

<u>Unknowns</u>

I dreamed of knowing.
Why in this life exist
thousands of living species,
so diverse and different?

Why so few people,
of life fully enjoy?
The majority busy with things
tribal or unnecessary,
most of his life.

Why can't we fly,
to know the earth?
If this is our home;
even it is from the air.

Why are we trapped
in four walls
and many times so happy we feel?

Why if being awake we dream,
aware of our dreams,
we rarely achieve them?

I dreamed that fair and unfair,

like oil on water,

it always floated.

But, although on the water if it did float,

as the foam it did it

and its existence very short

and insufficient it seemed to us

<u>Life</u>

Life is joy,
seasoned with tears and sorrows.
Life is surrounded
by many satellites,
different in each person,
and to each person marks
the same as their DNA.

Place of birth.
Family from which you descend.
Cultural and economic level
of the country and the family.
They will mark our destiny
whether we want it or not.

Knowing and discovering
a goal, may be
that to others goals in life will led us,
while we had freedom of choice
and a changing brain,
who guide us.

Dreams

If I were ethereal and could
steal to the evil its being.
If with the mind and its strength
I could make a dream world,
where the word happiness didn't exist
because within all living being will inhabit,
consubstantial to his being.

If to double intentionality
than with the words,
many times is played
to manipulate ideas,
in the air they will disintegrate
like sugar with heat.

If the invisible to the visible will eclipse,
letting see only the essence of things.

If the force of love
will pull down the frontiers
and in bridges of adhesion
and friendship, they would become.

<u>Cycle</u>

A child begins his life in a street any.

His parents on either side,
a hand they hold him.

With his two hands tightly linked
the streets are going passed.

The more streets he goes walking,
more weakly to the hands he takes holds.

Until, little by little,
the young man walks the streets alone.

Many years have passed,
many streets he has transited.

The young man has become
a mature man.

His strong and responsible hands
are now the ones that hold,
those of his elderly parents.

To keep traveling more streets,
until his hands
are left alone again,
and to his memories they were grabbed.

Visibility

The day runs and advances,

while the light, to him guides,

along different paths.

After walking his way,

tired and exhausted,

in the dark, he rests.

The night with its mantle

to him it covers

and hides to the predators.

The day, with its renewed strength,

its power increases,

to the darkness, dazzles,

and its invisibility prevents.
Thus, another cycle in its path, it travels.

If visibility to the invisible, hides

as the day to the night

Won't it be the no-visible part,

the mantle that cares and wraps,

to the visible and dazzling part we know?

Contributing

A person walks day by day
and when the sunset
closes her eyes, she rest.

Section by section,
he goes tracing her path.
Sometimes she perceives
beyond what her eyes can see,
adding creativity,
empathy and hope,
to her objective reasoning.

If in her tiny world,
as objective is set,
improve something inside
of her human smallness,
that to someone it benefits
and brings her joy.

If this little idea
into a good virus will be transformed
and will spread throughout the world?

Eternal childhood

She lived playing and dreaming,
she always floated,
never her feet was landed
on the ground.

Her look, from another dimension,
all things saw.
Never the harsh reality,
his thought reached,
she didn't even intuit her.

In her world she lived,
the earth like a ball she saw it,
within which she always
dreamed and played.

With a thousand things,
she entertained
and enjoyed them all.
Malice never in her life discovered her.

Idleness never knew

because curiosity eclipsed it.

Her mind always flew

to imaginary worlds

and always to those worlds of happiness,

she adapted,

living with all the beings

that inhabited those worlds.

<u>Footprints</u>

Wrinkles what the skin in its face shows us.
Unequivocal sign,
of a long time lived.
Footprints of suns by the skin absorbed,
over the course of a cycle,
repeated throughout a life.

Learning, what from children,
it forms to our brain
and you deepen its folds.
More years,
more experiences,
more knowledge,
in the furrows of the brain,
their unequivocal imprint,
they go leaving

Footprints of treads in the land we inhabit,
as furrows that we go leaving in it.
Faithful images
of the kind of life that has been taken,
and in each footprint marked, it's reflected.

<u>Feigning</u>

Feigning what you would like to be,

and hide what you really are.

Feigning to be an orange

when you're a lemon.

Feigning to be a flower when

you're a beautiful cactus.

To seem to be very clever

with falsehoods and deceptions,

for to be able to dazzle

with a false appearance;

what to others, it blinds

with my false enlightened self.

To appear to be very beautiful

with touches-up and artifices,

so that all the doors,

with only look at them,

in the face of your beauty, they open up.

More if, the doors once already passed,

in a transparent circle,

they'll isolate you,

from which you can't get out.

What would we do?

Feigning, locked in a bubble,

or live the reality.

<u>Objective</u>

A wonderful bird flies low.
Planning, go slowly,
its only objective,
is to find food to survive.

Once it has succeeded it,
the bird takes flight
and takes greater height.
Enjoying and appreciating
of its wonderful surrounding.

A strong and intelligent man
crawls on the ground.
His goal is not to find food
for your livelihood
since for many years
he has it guaranteed .

His wish is to achieve the wealth
and the power at all costs.
Sooner or later, what else does it matter!
Because his goal, he will achieve.
However it's very difficult for him,
who longer height, he takes
and his life at ground level
will always pass it.

<u>Advances</u>

A man with many years lived,
sitting at the door of his house,
the mind lets wander.

My eyes, every year,
they have less vision, he reflects.
Many neat images,
they have captured
over the years.

My hearing too,
has also lost its power,
the sounds, now,
I perceive them very weak.

My bones sore,
my figure has hunched over,
and without a cane, I fall.

My heart beats
very weak and unbalanced,
because a lot it has worked
throughout my life.

Today he turns years
and all his family is around him.

His older grandchildren,
in their eagerness by helping,
they make him good gifts.

One gives away him two eyes,
very easy to insert,
what will improve his vision.

Another gives away him a new
hearing system, of easy installation.

The third gives him
the latest technology.
A human framework
in which, he gets into,
and with a rechargeable battery,
step by step,
it take him wherever he wants.

The fourth gives away him a new heart,
which connects with to his,
and all his work, it performs,
as if he were a young person.

The man smiles gratefully
and thanks to everyone.
But when he only stays, he thinks,
Oh God! Why don't they give away me
the only thing,
what I really want and desire?

Silence

Silence that of the night
you make your abode,
that the moon is your north,
and the relaxation, you attract,
like honey to flies.

The dream in the silence leans,
and in the face of him, falls surrendered
and almost always succumbs.

Enemy you are of stimuli,
bustle, and hubbub,
that your peace very easily they alter.

Friend of calm, of rest,
which your silence, it prolongs,
expanding your strength.

Silence that the spirit you relax,
chasing away the noise,
so that the body rests
and its energy it renews.

Fragile silence that a cry breaks,

as if it was of fine crystal.

Laughter that after a silence,

in cry it has converted.

Silences that speak,

better than many words.

Words that, after a long silence,

they capture attention better,

reaching more into the heart or mind.

Why do we need of silence,

the same or more than food

that our body claims

with lesser or greater insistence?

What feeds

the silence

that is so

necessary?

Remembrance

Yesterday, a good man
this world, he inhabited.
His footsteps were leaving
a trace of goodness.

All his life,
to make a fairer world,
he was dedicated with firmness.

From humility
which in every human being resides,
with all his strength,
he tried to combat the meanness,
selfishness, indifference …

But the yesterday died,
and today, in the present we're.
This one today, orphan has remained.
From the yesterday,
we will always remain us his memory.

The traces that this good man,

on this earth, has left us,

will serve as an example for us;

to learn how it can dedicate

a whole life

to make a world more beautiful.

The depth of their footprints

will make, what for a long time,

other people follow them.

<u>Riddle</u>

My killer is going to be the same as yours.
He's going to be the cause of my death
and of yours as well.
Tells me my friend while
we chat, in the face of a cup of coffee.

And who is, I ask you?
I'll give you several clues,
and I'm sure, who you'll find out.

The same killer kills
to many people every day.

It doesn't matter where you reside,
on the five continents
the same killer acts.

He doesn't discriminate,
although he always prefers older people,
and sometimes not so older.

With these three clues
I'm sure you've already guessed.

– With a mocking smile, I answer.

– I only know his name,
which by - TIME -, we all call it.

And my friend answers me:
– Well, now he has surnames

– MORE POLLUTION –

<u>Perception</u>

On the top of a mountain,
from the deepest part of the earth,
a very strong, deep, vigorous voice,
all the letters of the alphabet,
she's proclaiming.

The diameter of its power is so large
that it reaches several countries.

It doesn't matter what language she speaks,
because everyone understands her.

The voice always
the same alphabet sings,
but each person in a different way,
captures it.

Some perceive only letters.
Others perceive different words.
And some several words,
forming sentences
with different meanings.

The space that sound travels.

The quantity of walls what it crosses.

The different winds

what to the voice they drag it.

The different sensibilities,

of the people who listen to it.

They will make the perception of some letters

multiply by one hundred,

and all of them different.

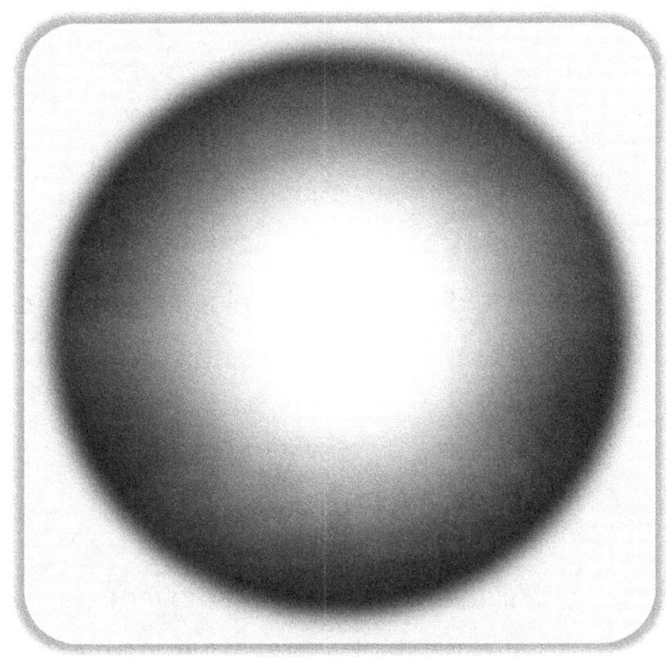

<u>Cleaning</u>

A huge roll of paper,

down an inclined street,

downhill, it was launched.

Metre to metre,

the street with the paper, was covered.

White and clean, the whole street remained.

All the people extoled

the whiteness of the street.

But one day a storm

with strong winds and hail,

all the paper shattered it.

The dirt, which the false whiteness covered,

with the paper, is mixed.

Agitated by a swirling wind,

all the dirt is piled up

All the dirt accumulated over time,

mixed with the false white paper,

in full view of all, it remained.

After the great failure

of hiding the dirt,

with a nice paper.

Every day, simple worker,

with a simple but effective machinery,

of clean up the streets,

they took care,

and the dirt day by day, they eradicated.

Ascending and descending

A ladder with only two steps
visible to the eyes,
well secured to the ground,
with a strong structure
of constancy and will,
a person possessed.

Every day of her life
the ladder used
and always higher she climbed.

The invisible steps
more and more grew,
as she used them.

Many times the steps, she descended
and the person learned, equal or more
that when she ascended.
If she stopped to think,
on why she descended.

But one day,
after a long time
of ascend and descend
for the invisible steps,
the person stopped climbing.

The stairway with the sky had joined
and from the earth this had disappeared,
leaving only the trace of its foundations,
which the earth absorbed.

Imagination

Imagination what to the reality
you increase or decrease it.
You even convert it, mold it or mix it.

Sometimes you magnify the real,
other on the contrary,
your negative exaggeration
to the reality in the underground
you bury it.

Imagination that from real images
you create other parallels ones
that, sometimes they integrate,
and other, they alone
they have a life of their own.

Imagination that to objective reality,
like the waves to the sea water,
a thousand shapes you make them adopt.
Sometimes its height
takes very high measures,
others are more manageable
and easy to get around.

Of one color you make a hundred

and its mixtures infinite.

Textures are changing

just like imagination is it,

that from a simple sheet of paper

a thousand forms it can creates.

From a single word,

the imagination gets a hundred,

that the sounds and the winds

will take charge of multiply

throughout of the times.

Running

The child runs behind the game,
just like he does behind love,
when he lacks it.

Runs the man behind the food,
when his organism demands it,
for their survival.

Runs the day behind night
or the night after day.
Sometimes the day runs more
and others the night extends its hours.

The man runs day by day,
as in a race,
until he reaches the finish line.

Each person runs their own career,
with very unequal assistance.
The differences between each person
will make unique every career.
The distances traveled
will not be the same either.

But the key question will be,
if the goal, once reached,
will also be different.

The stars run spinning;
Runs the Earth, the Sun, the Moon,
and all the planets...
One way or another;
it seems that everything is moving forward.

The question is;
Where does it all go?
Or simply the universe expands
until it reaches, we don't know
the What, the Why, nor the What for?

<u>Fragile</u>

If to the perishable.
like a pear that rots,
we consider fragile it.
If everything that expires,
because it has lost for its validity or
effectiveness,
we also say that it is fragile.

The adjective fragile to too many things,
we can put it on.

Fragile as a crystal, that with a blow
in a thousand pieces it breaks.

Fragile or helpless as a baby
who if does not receive food and care,
your life in a short time goes out.

Fragile as snowflakes;
which with a simple footstep,
from the ground disappear.

Fragile as the lie,
that when it gets too long, it breaks.

Fragile as a simple leaf;
That to the rhythm of the wind, it sways.

Fragile as the smoke of a cigar,
which immediately it disappears.

Fragile as a curtain of dust,
that a blow frighten it,
and she runs scared.

Fragile as foam,
that a minimum pressure,
it eliminates.

Fragile and defenceless as a plant,
which if not is irrigated,
it withers and dies.

Fragile as a dream;
which it is almost always forgotten.

Fragile as memory;
which throughout life,
many things, it goes forgotten.

Fragile as a fruit ripe;
which almost always it rots.

<u>Illusion</u>

Illusions that, sometimes,
illuminate a life,
like the sun illuminates
a new day.

Illusions, that to a child,
they give joy
and his childhood cheer his up
and stimulate.

Illusion for something concrete,
which many times,
it serves as stimulus
to reach new goals.

Illusions that happiness provide
in people's lives
though is momentary.

Illusions what feel as true,
knowing in advance,
that they are rarely fulfilled.

Illusions, that to the objective reality,
makes us perceive it
in a very subjective way,
because immediate satisfaction produces.

Illusions that while they are felt,

the hope increases,

mixing in the people,

the illusion with hope.

Illusion in the tomorrow,

that something new will bring us

if we desire it

with love, hope and enthusiasm;

just like a child does it.

<u>Manipulate</u>

The wind, at its whim,
to the clouds manipulates
in the direction in which it blows.

He inclines the branches of the trees,
according to the direction,
which at that moment it brings.

According it is their strength,
the branches, more bends them,
and the clouds faster it moves.

Some parents, with their attitudes,
manipulate conscious or unconscious,
to small children.

The lies to the truth,
like the wind to the clouds,
often manipulate it.

 A gardener to the plants that he takes care of,
with better or worse success,
manipulates them;

Interested propaganda

that she always manipulates

with the sole purpose of selling,

showing only the brightness and colorfulness;

keeping out all shadow,

which to the light can eclipse.

As a day that lacks darkness,

or a night that the artifice of the lights

for a day want to sell us.

<u>Tears</u>

Tears that fall unintentionally
when something affects us,
in a direct or indirect way,
and nothing we can do.
The impotence to see something sad,
unjust, that affects our heart,
and to our mind, it blocks;
and in the form of tears it is expressed,
to relax our body;
in the face of our inability to find a solution.

Tears that wet our faces
when an uncontrollable laugh,
in a natural way with any event,
many times very simple or banal,
from our eyes sprout, jointly with our laugh.

Tears of joy, of helplessness, sadness,
as if, at the falling,
the sensitivity towards a better world,
they could, make it be born,
and a first step, tear to tear,
they could create, to keep advancing.

Grandparents

Selfless love
that flows from their hearts
and in children
it will be embedded forever.

Infinite kindness before everything
that surrounds children, games, learning,
other children ... and his safety and happiness
preserve it.

One or a thousand hours,
of absolute dedication;
without asking anything in return,
with joy and humor.

Stars that always give a bright light
and that, throughout the children's lives,
will guide them.

Fine, constant and relaxed rain
that makes that children's lives,
little by little, are growing
with security and strength.

Eyes that capture
much more than they see,
and to the grandchildren
they are transmitted it,
with imagination and creativity
that their minds stimulate.

Wisdom that day after day they bring,
after many years lived,
 what their experience, they will provide them,
to face their future.

<u>Bridges</u>

Bridges what rise above the rivers,
like crowns of kings.

Trees and vegetation
that grows along the river,
with the humidity of the earth
which the river provides it.

Bridges what always have the purpose
of joining two strips of land,
by the river separate.

Rivers like mirrors that capture what they see
and their image reflects it.

Bridges that eliminate the frontiers
that the river bed forms.

Bridges reflected on
the crystalline waters of the river,
duplicating its image.
Floating on its channel,
joining the real with the illusion that,
when contemplating its beauty, it is created

Positivity

Positivity, like what the sweet,

warm, and soft sunlight

which in the darkness it is embedded

and in clarity it becomes it.

Positivity, like what a sad and poor meal,

with a mixture of color

and different textures,

in a delicacy it becomes.

Positivity, like what the calm waters of a river,

in life and wealth

from several villages it become .

Positivity, that good magnifies

and extends, like seeds with water;

and the bad diminishes and shrinks,

like seeds without water.

Changes

If is mixed the water with the earth,

and from its fusion the mud appears.

If we add straw or fiber

to the earth and water,

we will obtain adobe to make bricks.

If the iron with carbon is mixed,

a new element emerges,

baptized with the name of steel.

Other times of the mixtures

no new elements emerge,

only an increase of the volume,

which its sum facilitates.

From the mixtures often

arise new creations,

new materials,

new works,

variety, diversity,

differences, with a common base.

Also, sometimes
their essence is modified
for better or for worse.

Changes that through time,
have been done and will be done.

Advances, that the curiosity
and creativity discover
decade by decade.

The ways of life are changing
and people's brain,
in turn, it is adapting to new types of life.

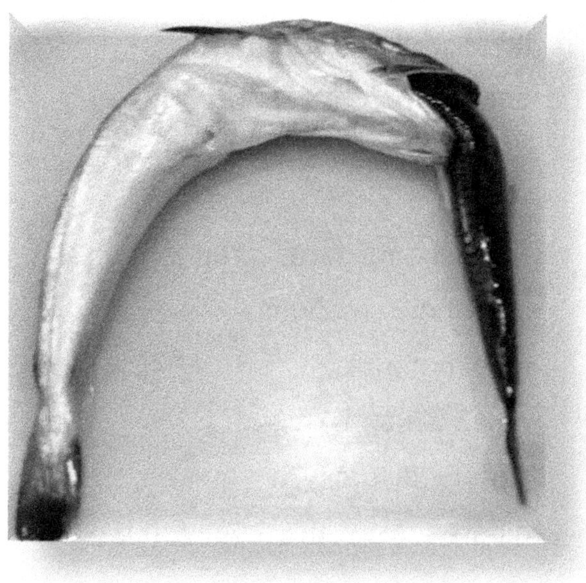

Rain and Words

Rain than your sound,

just like language it does,

your tone you changes,

depending on the weather

and circumstances.

Sometimes strong, angry, violent,

depending on the wind that is blowing

and the temperature that reigns

on the earth you discharges.

Your speed increases

and the sound you raise it up;

as it is does with words,

which from the throat sprout,

and through the mouth are thrown

when hate, the anger and rage

are their parents.

However, other times the rain,

soft, relaxed, unhurried,

on earth it descends,

like balm that soothes the skin.

Just like a poetic language,

which flows very smoothly

and with the air it is integrated,

so that it spreads throughout the world.

Like rainwater,

which is impregnated with the earth,

creating a circle of life

or a rain of words.

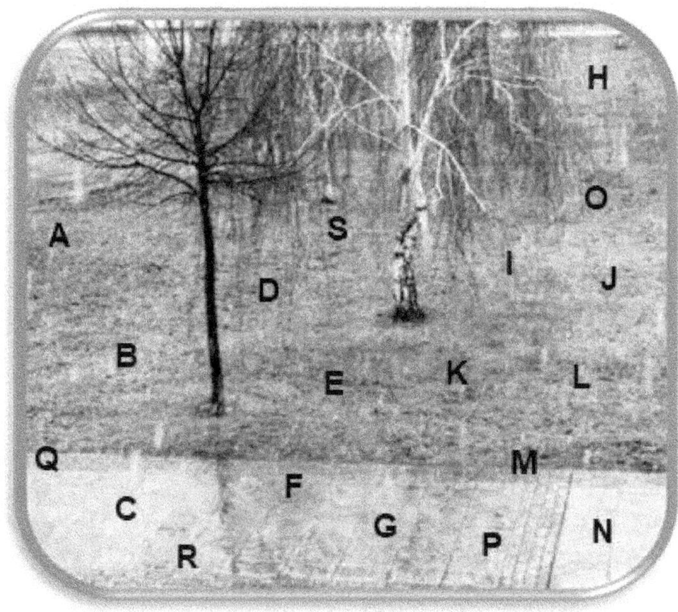

Choice or Manipulation

A person walks,

for a straight path.

She walks relaxed, she doesn't think,

nothing has to decide.

Alone with herself, happy and calm,

she's enjoying of the walk.

More after a while,

the path is divided into three.

She has to decide,

follow the straight path,

turn to her right,

or turn to her left.

The person stops and thinks

which path to choose.

Her brain starts to work.

Weighing the advantages that each path brings,

and the inconveniences and difficulties

that each election will bring.

The effort and work
who traveling every path
to her would suppose;
united to the benefits
that each one would bring.
Her brain is at full performance
to be able to decide.

Suddenly, all her attention
is absorbed by one of the options.
The path is full of light and music.
Many posters with attractive propaganda
to its borders are shown;
that invite you to buy and enjoy.

Images with people,
who have traveled that same path,
with smiling, happy, cheerful faces.

The brain stops working
because the person has already decided
and that's the path he chooses.
Without knowing nor weighing,
the reason of the election.

Time

Yesterday no longer exists,
it has volatilized,
it has become a dream
and in the world of memories,
it has been installed.

His recovery, although feasible,
is difficult, because the yesterday
changing like the clouds,
with a thousand shapes,
textures and colors,
it can be.

The tomorrow is planning,
sometimes it's a vision,
other times simply an illusion,
a lightning bolt of light,
or a deafening thunder.

The tomorrow is hope
when in the today there isn't it.
Making it more bearable,
or simply better.

The hope increases
the energy and desires,
with the will and the decision of,
the destiny to change.

When today is positive,
its duration is very short.
If the today is negative,
although its duration is the same,
longer will be made us.

If yesterday's memory is positive,
the today we will enjoy more.
If yesterday's memory is negative,
the today least brilliant will seem to us.

The TOMORROW,
from the TODAY is planned,
always keeping in mind
the memories of the YESTERDAY.